MOON CIRCLE

Rediscover wildness, intuition and sisterhood

By Lucy AitkenRead

Also by Lucy AitkenRead

Happy Hair - the definitive guide to giving up shampoo
30 Days of Rewilding - find your place in nature and
watch your family bloom
Freedom Face - a beauty guide free from toxic
ingredients, expensive gloop and self-hating bullshit

Contents

Introduction

We sat around a fire on one of the darkest nights of the year. It was freezing and I was melting the toes of my boots by holding them too close to the flames, but I needed the warmth and I was feeling an almost reckless abandon to the moment. There were eight of us sitting on a mixture of wonky camp chairs and logs, and we were shrouded in the heavy darkness of a moonless night.

We were speaking, just a short sentence each, whatever came out on our misty breath, but a picture was being woven from our words. It was an image of women filling the meadows between our fire and the river: they were wading into the river and being drawn into the sea; they were dancing and singing, filling the mountainside with their voices. Their faces were turned to the night sky, they threw their arms around each other, and laughed and roared. They were being ferociously themselves and they were boldly together. There were crowds of them, but they moved as one: they had a purpose, a shared dream, they were making it happen.

(We didn't know what "it" was. But whatever it was, they were crushing it. And as we sat around the fire we knew it was to do with us.)

Our words hung on the frosty air. We were startled at the picture we'd painted: the story we'd told accidentally but with mastery, as though we were Poetry Slam champs.

Although we'd begun our Moon Circle as novices,

Introduction

without knowing what we were doing (only a great sense that we needed it), somehow, drawn out of our collective subconscious, had come the perfect picture.

For by meeting together on a New Moon we are reclaiming our power as women; we are purposefully stepping into the river of womanhood that has twisted and turned throughout herstory. At times this river has cascaded deep under rocks, unseen, but still forming the earth. Other times it's thundered over landscapes, carving out new valleys.

Our Moon Circle is where we tell our stories to each other, where we take the sting out of the shame we've experienced, where we share tears over our griefs, and where we honour and bolster the dreams of each other's hearts.

It's a place where we know we belong, because we've seen each other's shadows and we're unafraid.

It's a place where we practise trusting ourselves, speaking on instinct, and voicing our intuition - and then we see that trust bleed out of the Moon Circle, flooding our everyday lives.

I've written this little book because, almost every week for a year, I felt I wanted to respond to various women in a hundred different circumstance with the words "Oh! You need a Moon Circle!". It's all very well to think everyone should get to have one, but another thing for people to actually go out and make one happen. So I'm sharing our story: how we got our Circle off the ground; and all the things we do as part of it.

A Moon Circle is for you if you've ever struggled with a sense of belonging. It's for you if you've ever been shamed or

Moon Circle

rejected, or made to feel small. It's for you if you feel you want to nourish your soul, but don't want to be part of a religious institution. It's for you if you have anger and hurt, and you need to vent in a safe place. It's for you if you feel an urge to connect to the earth, but feel at a loss about where to begin. It's for you if you have become skeptical of the 'women-are-bitchy' myth. It's for you if you are tired of being respectable and acceptable. It's for you if you feel a sense of something burning within you, and you want to stoke that flame.

I invite you to get comfy (perhaps not on a wonky log with a campfire melting your boots) while I tell you a little about my Moon Circle journey.

My first time

"Women's Circle in the forest! Bring something to sit on!"

My youngest daughter was asleep in the sling, her body pressed against my chest, my nipple still in her mouth. Tim was somewhere with Ramona, our eldest: they'd disappeared into the hall an hour ago. We were newly arrived in New Zealand from London, living in a bus that we'd driven on an especially tremulous whim to this homeschooling camp. Our children still had yonks to go before they were close to formal education age. But we were there. And we were in a strange zone of feeling that these were our people, but still having to go through the awkward ritual of making friends with them.

I didn't know what was happening in the forest, but I could see women all over the camp checking their kids were occupied, and pulling blankets out of their tents.

"In for a penny, in for a pound" I thought to myself as I grabbed a thin foam bed roll. At least if I bring this thing that looks like a yoga mat, they might think I do yoga.

I willed my legs into the forest. Some days I feel so shy. I'd rather avoid new experiences and new people, and just sit in a quiet corner reading a book. But we'd left all of our friends behind in England, and I knew we'd better crack on with finding some new ones.

I could see ten women in a clearing up ahead, and I focused on a little gap in the Circle where I dropped my mat, and folded myself onto it without waking Juno. I peered out above her head, catching the eyes of the women and smiling my bravest smile. There were other babies in slings, and mamas with tired eyes, and mamas that looked like they did yoga every day. There were older women, and a couple of women that didn't look old enough to have children at all.

I had no idea what was about to happen, and definitely no idea that what was about to happen would eventually become one of the things I most treasured in my life.

There was little introduction. The last stragglers joined the Circle and the shuffling eased, and then one of the older women confidently welcomed us and proposed we simply go around the Circle - how about clockwise? I quickly counted the women between me and her. Seven. Pheeeeew. I'd get a sense of what I was meant to do by the time it was my turn.

Well. By the time it was my turn I still had no clue about what I should say. Some women had just introduced themselves and spoken a little about their family and their work, as though we were at a business meeting or a La Leche League thing. And then one mother told us a huge story: ten or fifteen minutes hearing about her great grandmother. It was an intriguing, sinister tale. Another mother began to speak, but instead of speaking she just wept, and in between sobs told us that she was finding things really hard - too hard. Someone on her left placed a hand on her shoulder, but everyone else just looked on, apart from the others that cried quietly too.

I didn't get it. I totally didn't get it. My belly was flipping over. I felt sad for her, but also I felt like I was the wrong person to be bearing witness to such bold emotion. Weren't we mostly strangers? Doesn't she have a friend she could quietly weep to? Am I meant to cry? I don't feel like crying. I feel stone cold

My first time

awkward!

When the Circle came round to me I turned to the method some others had: I went in for 'business meeting', and I used the moment to tell them about my passions and hobbies. Perhaps, if I tell them I like respectful parenting and also making things out of stuff I find in the junk shops, they'll like me? I wasn't at all sure that's what these women were there to hear, but surely we weren't there to hear the deepest darkest confessions of each other's hearts?

Tim asked me about it later. "I can't tell you what was said, 'cos what is said in Circle stays in Circle. But it was, er.... intense. People cried. And I guess it was cathartic. But I don't know what the point was."

What is the point?

When women come together and make a commitment to each other to be in a circle with a spiritual center, they are creating a vessel of healing and transformation for themselves, and vehicle for change in their world.[1]

~

A year passed. We stayed in touch with the families from the camp, and many of them have become our besties here in New Zealand. The circle experience completely exited my mind. I didn't think about it much at all, apart from seeing it as an example of 'different strokes for different folks'.

How I chuckle at this now!

One day I was reading an incredible blog post by Bethany Webster, about[2] the way mothers pass down their wounds from daughter to daughter. I was in a turbulent time with my own beautifully wild spirited daughter. She is a majestic wonder, a whirlwind, a freight train, a canary in the gold mine making sure adults know that the way we treat children is not good enough! I was learning so much every day, but I was often surprised by the anger I found bubbling in my chest. I was afraid she would bear the brunt of scars I was carrying.

My face was wet with tears as I scrolled down the page, finding sentence after sentence ringing with resonance.

What is the point?

"Mothers may unconsciously project deep rage towards their children in subtle ways. **However, the rage really isn't towards the children.** The rage is towards the patriarchal society that requires women to sacrifice and utterly deplete themselves in order to mother a child."

I became aware that on a deep, subconscious level I was actually jealous of my daughter. Jealous of the way she is fully able to be 100% herself. Jealous of the way she expresses her massive emotions with her whole body and voice and every drop of energy. Jealous of the freedom in which she occupies her place in the world, without apology.

It's a huge word, jealousy.

It doesn't mark our relationship in a big way. It's not like when I was 14 and jealous of my best friend for getting to go out with the boy we had both fancied for two years. We used to have competitions about how much we fancied him; "I love him so much I would steal one of his sweaty socks and sleep with it on my pillow" and I'd say "Well I would eat his bogies!" - and now she is his GIRLFRIEND? I was consumed with this whole body ache. I'd wake up jealous and go to sleep jealous, and in between times think about his bogies, jealously.

It's not like that with my daughter.

We are deeply connected, we shower each other in kisses, we laugh until we cry, we play hard. But every so often, when I am analysing the moment that I exploded into a shout after asking her to stop doing something seven gazillion times, I discover that the blast came out of a subterranean place within my heart.

Moon Circle

Bethany Webster's blog post named it for me: a mother's wound. I knew it was so! A mother's wound - the pain women carry from years of having to fulfil certain roles and expectations - can leave us feeling like we are not quite good enough, or that there is something wrong with us, or that we must be a certain way to be loved. Or it can leave us feeling plagued by guilt for wanting more than we have.

Some days I felt that wound as a throbbing sore: a pain that kept making me want to lash out at my children, simply for being so ferociously free.

I read on:

"In our society, there is no safe place for a mother to vent her rage."

My eyes locked on to the words "a safe place for a mother to vent her rage" and I knew with a concrete certainty that the place I would do this would be a Moon Circle. I didn't even think of that first circle of women in my mind at the time, so quickly had it left my mind, but now I know it has planted a stealthy, staunch seed. The sentence rang in my mind for days, and I began thinking about who might want to join me in venting our rage, giving space to voice our disappointments, and perhaps taking an opportunity to step more fully and freely into who we truly are.

That week I took the first step towards being part of a Moon Circle.

Something along the lines of...

The grass was wet and the wood was damp. It was a good job I'd started in plenty of time, because this fire did not want to be lit! It would catch and then go out, and then I'd have to get on my knees again and blow until I was purple to help it flare up. Tim came down from our yurt 100 metres away to see if I needed a hand with getting it going, I shooed him away. "I can light a flipping fire. Gah." Ten minutes later I flapped in to the kitchen, rummaging in the drawer for fire lighters.

I shoved some under the kindling and within a few minutes I had a roaring blaze, I checked my phone. Just in time, the women will be arriving any second. I pushed at the smoke, hoping the chemical pong of the fire lighters would leave before everybody settled in around the fire. That pong was exposing my lack of wild woman credentials! My neighbour was as keen as me to get this Moon Circle happening, and as we co-own some beautiful meadows and woods, we'd invited everyone to our place. She was waiting at our gate and I joined her, praying the fire would stay lit. Cars pulled in and we hugged everyone as they stepped out.

These were the courageous women who had responded to my out of the blue and unclear email! The neighbours on each side of our farm, a potter from down the river, a landscape gardener from the other side of the mountain, a mama from town, and another couple of women that we didn't know very well but just had a good feeling about. Looking back on it now I really can't believe they turned up! Just so you are completely aware of how vague I was about what we were going to do, here is the exact email I sent them:

Moon Circle

"Hope you are well! Just a quick one to see if you would be interested in coming along to a women's moon circle we are hoping to start? The first one will decide what sort of thing it will be, but at this stage probably something along the lines of sharing our stories/joys/hurts around a campfire. Might you be interested?"

My neighbour and I had spent some time thinking about how we would begin our Circle. I'd been reading a lot about "men's circles" as my husband was in one, and I was aware they often used ritual to mark out the Circle as sacred. Throughout my life I have appreciated how candles and symbolism can make me more mindful and help me feel completely present and whole. I well understood how important small actions could be in opening our hearts and helping us set aside any natural cynicism, so we'd had a little talk about the things we might do to set the scene.

We'd decided we would lead our other neighbours, friends and friends-to-be on a silent walk to the fire. As we stood by the cars my neighbour explained that as we walk across the meadow we were to be aware of what we are feeling, the thoughts in our mind and the tension in our body. That first silent walk felt unusual and beautiful. I was almost giddy with this strange sense of wide open, unknowing, potential.

Once at the fire, we asked everyone if they would like to be "smudged", which involves lighting herbs and moving the smoke across people's bodies. Sage has been used in different cultures throughout history to clear the air in this way. The smell is evocative and, as we stood in silence, it helped me feel even more present.

Something along the lines of...

We settled in around the fire, barely smouldering now due to my neglect (or due to being present to the silent walk and smudging, of course!) I spent the first few minutes of the circle making myself feel faint by blowing on the embers. We had a chuckle at the dense smoke wafting around us, and I held in my need to spill all the drama of lighting the bloody thing.

I welcomed everyone. I was truly grateful that they had turned up. I explained how we didn't have a strong picture of what this group would look like, or what we would do, but that we had some ideas and we were very much open to the ideas of other participants. We went around the Circle, and each women shared what her needs were and what she hoped to get out of the Circle.

It was the beginning of a great, mysterious adventure for us all, and at the time we didn't know we were tapping into a model of being together that women have used in the most powerful ways for hundreds of generations. These women were to become my Moon Sisters.

Wayfaring

We've been meeting in this way for a year and a half now, and when the eight of us sit around our fire on the new moon it does feel like we are rekindling some ancient, primitive behaviour: the gathering around the one safe place in the wild.

Earlier this year we held a women's retreat: two nights away in an old Scout camp. It was a time for people to reflect, be quiet, and take some time just for themselves. We had some powerful circles led by my friend, who's been a part of a Moon Circle on the coast for ten years. Their circle begins at 9pm, and goes through the night until after dawn. They might get a chance to head home before the school run, or they might head straight into their day. The joy and fulfilment of the Circle buoys them, and they say their families love the day after Circle, as they are so soft and open.

In between women's retreat activities we found ourselves in the dorm, talking about why Circles are so powerful. It was the kind of conversation that fizzed with magic and mystery, like we were touching on old truths only just being revealed. I had a fluttering in my chest and tears in my eyes as we shared our ideas about how the act of women sitting together is a refusal to believe the myths we are told about how women relate to each other. It is the roaring of lions long dormant: it is a recognition of the deep, grounded power of womanhood.

My friend is Polynesian, and she described to me how traditionally the women in her culture met behind closed doors during menstruation in order to receive visions together. Others in the village honoured the closed doors and the sacred space, as the women would return to them bearing wisdom about the future. The female menstrual gathering provided wayfaring for the village.

I lit up as she spoke - it makes so much sense! So many women in touch with their menstrual cycle will be aware of how visionary the time of bleeding can be. If I take the time to be still - to shut down a little - I feel myself sparking with insights. If I can't hit pause during menstruation, I find myself frustrated, with this feeling of an itch I can't reach: truths lying under wraps all around me that I can't uncover.

If only it was the norm for all women to set themselves apart during menstruation in order to receive wisdom for the future. I doubt we'd be in this Trumpy mess!

It's rare now, too rare, but once we dig around a little we find that different elements of Moon Circles can be found throughout history.

In some cultures women gathered in moon lodges to bleed together. Sometimes it was an honour, a great privilege - and in other cultures they were forced there. The Nepalese tradition of Chaupadi is still common today, but it's the very worst of this separation: menstruating women are considered impure, and are forced to sit out their menstruation in extreme weather conditions, discomfort, and isolation. At the other end of the spectrum, a Hawaiian menstrual hut, Hale Pa'e, seemed to be a sacred community of women: a sanctuary with an emphasis on re-centering and relaxing during a woman's moon time.[3]

Evidence of gathering in circles has been found in ancient art on cave walls, and in the neolithic boulders scattered in perfect formation. Tribes still connected to an ancient way of life still meet in circle. But for many societies meeting in circle isn't much done. We gather in rows or in elbows-out scrums - settings where the first or strongest gets the best position. In a circle, space is made for every attendee, and every participant is equally.

Between the 1960s and 1980s women across the world began to meet in circle, recognising that this egalitarian form of meeting better represents an anti-patriarchal culture. In the early 2000s a group of women harnessed the internet to encourage women to sit in sister circles under the banner Gather the Women and more recently

The Red Tent, the 1997 novel by Anita Diamant, tells the biblical story of Dinah and builds a beautiful picture of what the pre-modern menstrual spaces could have looked like. Many women have been inspired by the novel, and are creating Red Tent spaces for women to gather and share stories and food in towns all over the world.

There are some beautiful modern expressions of menstrual lodges and sacred circles and when we sit in our own Moon Circle we feel like one thread in a rich tapestry that's been woven by women across generations and cultures.

Belonging

I'd known with an uncanny certainty that a Moon Circle would provide some of the healing I needed for the pain I carried. Almost immediately our Moon Circle became a salve for my mother's wound, despite seldom actually using the sharing time as a chance for a good ragey vent! More often than not I simply shared some thought process I was working through at that time, or a book I was being inspired by, an ambition I was hoping to fulfil, or a bizarre dream I was trying to analyse. I am surprised by how rarely I've had to share a story of parenting angst: it's almost as if simply sitting in circle is enough. It is a salve simply in and of itself.

To what end do we sit together under the moon? Why circle in together?

We sit to be heard. To speak without being judged. To share our stories without having to make an articulate point.

We sit to listen. To rekindle the ancient art of listening with open hearts. To know other women on a heart to heart level.

We sit to spill tears and laughter, and to hold on to a strong thread of silent solidarity.

We sit to see truth. To have parts of ourselves revealed to us. To have the stories of others laid bare. To hear words spoken that shoot into the heart like a lightning strike. To come to understand a wisdom unveiled in silence.

We sit to dig our toes into the cosmos. To be pulled into

Moon Circle

the expansive river of consciousness that we didn't know existed. To experience a oneness with humankind and the universe that feels like floating along on gentle rapids. We meet together to have our cynical minds opened by a shooting star's approving appearance, or to watch the clouds pass over the face of the moon and be flushed with the deep sense of belonging.

That sense of belonging is the most powerful thing. Feeling that we truly belong somewhere is one of humankind's most profound urges. As society becomes increasingly fractured, as our fences gain in height, as our local shop becomes a mall, as places of worship begin to feel out of touch, this urge just sits there, malevolently unmet. In the most tragic cases this lack of belonging becomes addiction, self-harm, or suicide. More commonly it is exists as an ache that we try to smother by consuming: fashion, media, gadgets, alcohol.

Small and intentional Circles can be a panacea for the loneliness that stalks us, and that the rage-venting, dream-sharing, heart-listening, and cosmos-digging are all the healing activities that happen once you know you truly belong.

Spirit

One Moon Circle last summer we passed around a small brown glass bottle of tincture made from the native Koromiko plant. As we each placed a drop on our tongues the beautiful woman who bought it along described how this essence was related to intuition and tranquility. She shared how inspired she was by the course she'd recently begun about the relationship between native plants and our souls. I loved hearing her describe her new knowledge of the plants, and as she described her awakening, how this plant wisdom were given her a new understanding of herself, I thought of Mechthild of Magdeburg's quote;

> *"The day of my spiritual awakening was the day I saw and knew I saw all things in God and God in all things."*

It's a theology that had always quickened my spirit, but I'd denied it since being a good student at Bible college age 19. As my friend spoke I found myself nodding, yearning for the same, and knowing with certainty that God could be found in the golden veins that run across the skeletal frame of an old mahoe leaf.

A spirituality connected to the plants that live around us? I am so on board with that.

My Moon Sister who was telling her story is no bold spiritual guru: she's a gardener with a soft voice and a warm smile. But as she shared so authentically, and as we passed the tincture around it felt like communion.

Moon Circle

There tends to be an inescapable reverence in a Moon Circle, even for those who don't align themselves with any particular spirituality. The ritual, the singing, and the deeply authentic way of being with each other can give Circles a cathedral-like quality. I have come to believe that regardless of women's spiritual persuasion, Moon Circles are relevant and powerful.

In the spirit of sharing opening, truthfully, and vulnerably, I thought I might tell you a little of my own spiritual experience.

I had a fairly traditional, evangelical Christian upbringing. I sat happily on the lefty, progressive, activist side of this spectrum for years. I'd always thought it was simply unfair that all of Christianity's main characters were men, but when I became a mother I realised it was actually wrong. Of course God isn't a man! Having daughters made me staunch in my decision to refer to God as Her and She- and it has meant my girls have often come home from relatives' homes saying "They think God is a MAN!" in an incredulous tone.

Over the last few years I've become increasingly skeptical of any patriarchal spirituality, and have been quietly dismantling much of my learned spirituality. I've come to understand that there are far more ways to the Divine then I could ever imagine, and I've heard the voice of God answer me through a mountain, and through the paths a raging river wore on the banks.

"Restoring the feminine symbol of deity means that divinity will no longer be only heavenly, other, out there, up there, beyond time and space, beyond body and death. It will also be right here, right now, in me, in the earth, in this river

Spirit

*and this rock, in excrement and roses alike. Divinity will be in
the body, in the cycles of life and death, in the moment of decay
and the moment of lovemaking.* [4]

I think it would have been a bit disruptive, a bit scary, if
I didn't feel so held by the sacred feminine, and, in particular, the
deeply sacred encounters with the other women in my Moon
Circle.

I haven't felt bereft, as I'd assume someone would when
they leave so much of their religion behind: I've only ever felt
curious and excited by the new imagery and words arriving at
my doorstep. Every time I read something about the divine
feminine, or someone shares something about their experience of
earth spirituality, my soul leaps as though it recognises it - as
though it's been smothered all this time by Man Religion.

It's like I'm the princess who has been lying on ten
mattresses, only just becoming aware of the pea. And the pea is
delicious, not annoying - and all around me are other princesses
munching on their yummy midnight pea.

There is always such a potent sense of healing, and I
leave the Circles feeling so replenished and whole that I've no
doubt in my mind that they are divine - that God is in it all. But
you might not feel comfortable with that: you might prefer me to
write Higher Power, Gaia, The Universe, Mother Earth, or
Buddha. And do you know what? That totally works. I'm not
being dismissive, or suggesting that it's all just semantics: I'm
saying that these Circles are strong enough to hold the beliefs of
all the women present - they are so encompassing and so
expansive that a Circle can bind us all in healing.

22

Moon Circle

I've only ever been in one or two Circles where language was dominated by a specific spirituality. More often that not they are wide open, and able to be interpreted by the spiritual beliefs of each individual participant. I encourage you to keep your rituals and language simple and undogmatic: let your Circle be a place dominated by freedom, sisterhood, and healing, rather than any one specific religion.

And if you feel you can't authentically bring a spiritual element in to your Circle, how about trying some reverent agnosticism?

"I'm now a reverent agnostic. Which isn't an oxymoron, I swear. I now believe that whether or not there's a God, there is such a thing as sacredness. Life is sacred. The Sabbath can be a sacred day. Prayer can be a sacred ritual. There is something transcendent, beyond the everyday. It's possible that humans created this sacredness ourselves, but that doesn't take away from its power or importance."[5]

Ritual

*We do spiritual ceremonies as human beings in order to
create a safe resting place for our most complicated
feelings of joy or trauma, so that we don't have to haul
those feelings around with us forever, weighing us down.
We all need such places of ritual safekeeping. And I do
believe that if your culture or tradition doesn't have the
specific ritual you are craving, then you are absolutely
permitted to make up a ceremony of your own devising,
fixing your own broken-down emotional systems with all
the do-it-yourself resourcefulness of a generous plumber/
poet.*[6]

~

I have come to love sacred rituals. Even the small act of
lighting a candle or burning some oils can rest my soul, and tell
my mind that something new is going to happen.

We use rituals in our Moon Circle in order to set the
evening apart as a sacred space. We use it to recentre ourselves,
to allow crashing thoughts to melt away. Like music and art,
rituals can open our hearts to new possibilities. They allow us to
see with a fresh clarity, and bring us to a space of liminality.
Liminal space is what we feel when we see a stunning sunset and
the world around us drops away. It's when we hear a new song
and begin crying at the traffic lights. It's the quiet of Christmas
Eve, when everything is done and all the family is asleep, and

Moon Circle

your mind grows still and full of gladness.

Richard Rohr[7] a Christian contemplative, describes liminal space as this:

"where we are betwixt and between the familiar and the completely unknown. There alone is our old world left behind, while we are not yet sure of the new existence. That's a good space where genuine newness can begin. Get there often and stay as long as you can by whatever means possible...This is the sacred space where the old world is able to fall apart, and a bigger world is revealed. If we don't encounter liminal space in our lives, we start idealizing normalcy. The threshold is God's waiting room. Here we are taught openness and patience as we come to expect an appointment with the divine Doctor."

Rituals bring us there. They shake off the normal and mundane, and take us to a place of transcendence.

I'm often struck by how many of the rituals and activities of our Moon Circles reference the four salves, an ancient understanding of the elements that are important for our well-being.

"In many shamanic societies, if you came to a shaman or medicine person complaining of being disheartened, dispirited, or depressed, they would ask one of four questions.

When did you stop dancing?

When did you stop singing?

When did you stop being enchanted by stories?

When did you stop finding comfort in the sweet territory of silence?

Where we have stopped dancing, singing, being enchanted by stories, or finding comfort in silence is where we have experienced the loss of soul.

Dancing, singing, storytelling, and silence are the four

Ritual

universal healing salves."[8]

Here are some rituals we often turn to, choosing just one or two to set the sacred space. Any more than that and it moves from being simple to being complicated.

Silent walk

We meet at the cars, hug everyone, and wait for people to turn up. Then we remind everyone about our sacred silent walk, and we ask everyone to be silent until we sit. We ask people to do a body scan, to see where they are holding tension, and to allow their thoughts to drift around their bodies and their anxieties. And then we walk silently to the fire. We walk slowly. We resist the urge to giggle. These three minutes of silence allow us to arrive calmly at the fire.

Smoke cleansing

The act of burning herbs, often referred to as smudging, has been used throughout history as a form of purification. First Nations people burn sage as a sacred, ceremonial act to cleanse the air. High Anglicans burn incense in church as a remnant of the ancient practice of burning incense in temples and home, to get rid of awful smells when someone important comes over. We generally burn dried sage that our neighbour grows, but have burned native branches of totora, rosemary, and lavender. Other things also have cleansing properties: particularly cedar and sweet grass. Sometimes we pass our smudging herbs from one to the other or sometimes one of the space holders moves around the people standing next to the circle, wafting the burning herbs around them. The person that tends to do the smudging in our Circle likes to send good thoughts out with the smoke or receive a word or picture from the person they are smudging- but don't put any pressure on yourselves to do this!

Moon Circle

Before long the smell of the herbs you burn can be enough to bring you into a liminal space in your own home, or in your own company. Sometimes if I am feeling anxious or restless I burn sage and do some deep breathing. It is a cue for me to lead from my soul. This is a small way in which the Moon Circle can nourish and nurture in the weeks in between Circles.

Candle lighting

Often our Circles begin with each woman sitting down and saying her name, and lighting a candle that she then places in front of her. As we light our candles we are marking ourselves as wholly present, and there is something precious about a circle of women, each with a shining light before them - a light they have lit themselves.

Leaving burdens

Sometimes we pass around a basket of stones. We each take one and share the burden that is weighing us down - something we don't want to focus on in the sharing circle, but something that is taking up space in our mind. We say what it is out loud, and we say "I'm going to leave it here, and pick it up later", and then we place the stone around the fire. Sometimes we remember to pick them up again, and sometimes we don't!

Resting our hands in water

This is a nice ritual for times when you have created a beautiful space inside a room for people to enter. Have a bowl of water at the door, and invite women to rest their hands in it, allowing the water to cleanse them and creating a clean slate for the evening.

Movement

Sometimes we begin our circle with some stretches or

yoga poses. Someone will guide it, using a meditative tone to suggest the pose. We might stretch out our arms like the trees, and sink our feet into the earth like roots. We might spiral our bodies and end in some free movement, making space for our bodies to stretch and shake in the way they need to. I love how quickly this kind of ritual can make me shed my inhibitions. I begin to feel myself living within every cell of my body, I stop caring about how I am seen through anyone else's eyes. It's a lesson in trusting my body all over again.

Ritualised introduction - matriarchal lineage

As people light their candle, or as the talking piece is first passed around the circle, people introduce themselves. At some circles the women will say their name and follow it up by honouring their matriarchal lineage, a line so often forgotten in history.

I say;

"I am Lucy, daughter of Anne. Granddaughter of Win Read and Betty Tribble, Great Granddaughter of Ivy May Humphries, Great Great Granddaughter of Mrs Norman"

I have loved how this has made me enquire after the undocumented women in my family history. It is something special to honour the line of women, and conjure up all the stories and cells that have led to me being where I am today. As we go around the circle, each woman speaking the names of the women of their line, it feels as though we are ushering in a host of saints to be present at our Moon Circle. I can almost see the women surrounding us, curious and protective, understanding that we are somehow healing the patriarchal rift that cast them adrift.

Ritualised introduction - menstrual cycle

In another circle we have introduced ourselves and shared where we are in our moon cycle. This seems like a very bold thing to do in a culture that buries our bleeding in shame and silence. It felt hugely liberating to declare out loud that we were ovulating, or bleeding, or premenstrual, or approaching ovulation, or menopausal, or pregnant. Then we shared how we were feeling within ourselves in relation to that. There are two additional benefits of doing this: it requires people in the Circle to be aware of their cycle, which creates a vital culture of women being present to their bleeding; and it can lend some understanding to what a person's needs might be, and what sort of space they are occupying.

Some circles then shift around, organising their seating position according to where they are in their cycle, moving from women who are bleeding, to those who have finished bleeding, to those approaching ovulation, to those who are ovulating, to those who have finished ovulating, to those approaching bleeding - who, of course, end up sitting next to the bleeders. This new seating plan can be a lovely way of honouring our cycles and placing importance on something held with such disregard outside of the Circle.

Discussion and deep heart sharing is important when deciding on what rituals and activities you might do. As an example, something like this acknowledgement of menstrual cycles might feel too hard for someone struggling with their new menopausal stage, or someone painfully trying to conceive, or a woman who doesn't have a menstrual cycle.

Guided meditation

There are many meditation resources available, and each

one has a different feel. If you are thinking of a Moon Circle with a theme, or a common spirituality, you might choose to use meditations from those origins. If someone in your Circle already leads yoga or meditation that can serve as a resource for the whole Circle, but if you don't have a person with that background in your Circle it can be just as powerful to have someone read a meditation out loud. When reading a guided meditation read it slowly, with a pause before each sentence, so people can absorb what is being asked of their imaginations.

One of the most amazing guided meditations that opened a Moon Circle was one by Jane Hardwicke Collings. The person that led the meditation used her own language, and you can bring your own language to this too - omitting or adding words to bring it more within your comfort zone.
With Jane's permission I share it with you here.

Grounding Exercise
This grounding exercise can be used at the start of any circle work. It calms, centres and connects everyone, and begins the creation of the group field. Sit in a circle, everyone holding hands – left palm up, right palm down, close eyes and focus on the breath.

Feel where you are touching the ground
And as if you are a tree, grow some roots down
See them going down through the layers of the Earth
Through any water, through the bones of your ancestors,
Deep, deep into the earth.
Reach for the Earth's centre
Wrap your roots around the golden core of the Earth
Draw up with your in breath the yin energy from the Earth
See the golden and healing energy travelling up through

Moon Circle

your roots
Then see your whole body fill with this energy
Repeat this process 3 times

Now take your awareness to the top of your head
Your crown chakra
Smile, this opens your crown chakra.
Send out branches, into the field of energy that surrounds
you
Reach up into the heavens,
Feel your connection with the universal energies.
Grow your leaves and turn them towards the Sun
Draw in the yang energy from the Sun
See the energy moving down through your leaves and
branches and filling your whole body,
Breathe it into you
Repeat this process 3 times

Bring your attention to your heart
Think of someone you love, this warms and opens your
heart, breathe deeply
See the yin Earth energy,
and the yang Sun energy swirling together at your heart
centre.

Bring your awareness into your whole body
Feel the Earth energy and the Sun energy
in your body, from the tip of your toes,
to your fingers and everywhere in between
Bring your awareness right here right now
Breathe deeply

Blessed Be.

Cultural Appropriation

There is a real danger of cultural appropriation when we sit in sacred circle. As white people across the world are waking up to these needs of the soul it can seem too easy to turn to cultures that still have powerful methods of meeting these needs. It is inspiring to see communities like the First Nations people using ancient knowledge to bring meaning and connection to their communities. It can be tempting to try and lift those more accessible practices and transplant them in to our communities and circles.

We are at our very best when we bring our own fresh ideas and creativity into our gatherings and Circles. I like to imagine that each Circle might bring their hearts and minds together to find new ways of being together, forming a sacred space, listening from the heart, and ritualising our experiences. But we are at our worst when we take from cultures that have a history of oppression and bend their rituals to our own ends, with no honouring or analysis of the injustice involved.

Of course, the genetic make up of any circle would likely represent many cultures, including indigenous cultures. In our Circle the dominant culture is Pākehā New Zealand, but there is also Māori, Indian, Irish and Welsh blood amongst us - cultures that all have some form of traditional of female gatherings.

It can be a beautiful thing to look through our own ancestral histories to see if there is anything we can be inspired from in our own Circles. There might be a meaningful word or phrase or object or notion that we can bring into our circle from our cultural heritage.

Sometimes Circles will feel a deep need to borrow from

another culture. I believe this can be done without being appropriative. If we are to borrow a practice from an indigenous culture it is so important to find out as much as we can about the tradition: to research it and understand as fully as we can what the ritual or object represents. And then we must honour the culture from which it is borrowed, to acknowledge the source that birthed the practice. I will share a good example of this in the chapter on the Talking Piece.

DIY ritual

The rituals I've discussed in this section are some that we've used in different Circles, but we also want to develop new ones, to create rituals that connect us and open our hearts and minds. I invite you to do the same. DIY rituals are the perfect alternative to appropriating the sacred rituals of other cultures. Use the rituals I've described as a jumping-off point and let your mind wander over what could make the perfect ritual.

Think about the purpose of the ritual. Is is transformation? Remembrance? Transcendence? Do you want to focus the Circle on a season, or on an intention? Can people do something with an object, or with their bodies? Are people picking something up, or casting something away? As a host, think about using surprise too: keep things under a scarf until it is time to reveal them. This stops them being a distraction, and can help us drop into the magical zone a little easier. Think about light, dark, and colour. Think about what objects can represent. Think about the elements: earth; fire; water; and air/ spirit. Think about the big, key moments in life that the women in your Circle might be experiencing.

Sharing

*As long as we share our stories, as long as our stories
reveal our strengths and vulnerabilities to each other, we
reinvigorate our understanding and tolerance for the little
quirks of personality that in other circumstances would
drive us apart. When we live in a family, a community, a
country where we know each other's true stories, we
remember our capacity to lean in and love each other into
wholeness.*[9]

~

The sharing circle is the guts of a Moon Circle. It's the
part where we rage into the night! I jest - sometimes there will be
rage, other times tears, and sometimes just the gentle sharing of a
tough time or a tender moment.

In a sharing circle everything spoken is confidential, and
everything is spoken with the understanding that there is no
judgement made and no advice required.

We sometimes begin with one simple round where
people share what is at the front of their minds.. They might
share a difficulty they are having at work, or a joy they have
found in their spring garden. Someone might immediately go
deep, and others might share in a similar vein, or head back into
their comfort zone and share something less personal.

Moon Circle

Eventually, either in the first round or the first evening together, or over several Moon Circles, the sharing circle becomes a place for immediate, vulnerable sharing. I often turn up knowing something I want to turn over in Circle - or, often, someone else's wounds will open up something in me.

Many women find that the thing they want to speak about throbs within them until it is said. Others don't know what they want to say until they say the words "I'm not sure exactly what I want to say..." Often, the Moon Circle feels so warm, inclusive, and open that people who might not normally share on this level find it easy to do so.

I like passing the talking piece around the group for this reason, rather than placing it back in the centre each time. It means you don't have to be a bold type of woman in order to get your hands on the talking piece! It just ends up in everyone's palms at one time or another.

You'd think I'd need to write here about honouring people's time and not flooding the Circle with one person's words, but do you know what? I have never sat in a Circle where that has happened. People have told long stories, and they have bounced from one grief to another and back again, but it has never been unwelcome. It has never felt out of place. In small groups of five or large groups of 12 there has always been enough time and enough grace in the Circle to simply hear everything people need to say. We all apologise, of course: "I'm sorry, I'm all over the place tonight..." or "I've been hogging the piece, I know, but I need to get this off my chest" - but in each Circle it's a different person who needs it.

Talking Piece

Our Moon Circles often include the use of a small, gnarled piece of wood. It's been softened by the river, and rubbed down by the women holding it. It's born witness to tears and laughter, and hundreds of stories of shame, and grief, and jubilation. It's our Talking Piece.

I have sat in circles with talking pieces, and without. It seems as though a talking piece really does transform the way we gather. I've come to believe a talking piece gives the vital element of structure to something that otherwise needs to be fluid. We are given permission to rest in the function of the talking piece!

The Talking Stick is a well known part of First Nations culture, it's almost a motif of peace. Some tribes use a stick, and others use different sacred objects. such as feathers. First Nations people use a talking piece in their circles to ensure impartiality. It is used in ceremonies and discussions, to settle disputes - whenever a group needs to communicate with each other.

The talking piece is not just an object, but a philosophy. It is about speaking and listening from the heart. When we sit in circle we simply listen with our whole selves, without our analytical mind wanting to ask questions or offer judgement. We withhold our advice and opinions. We listen as though there are ears stuck on our heart. And we speak from the heart too. We don't sit and think about the awesome wit with which we will tell our story. We don't fret about what we are going to say, or conjure up the ideal way to package our problem so we come across in the best light. We listen and listen and listen, and then the talking piece comes into our hands and we speak from our heart.

Honestly! The things I have SAID in circle! Ha. There has been so much spilling of guts! I never regret what I have spoken about, but it is so far from the measured speech I'd usually attempt in order to come across as wise and humorous! And it's awesome, because I get to be completely vulnerable without receiving any unwanted opinion or advice - which I hate getting at the best of times, let alone when I am being all bare and open.

As you can imagine, the Talking Stick is an incredibly powerful tool, and there are many First Nations people who willingly offer the concept for non-indigenous groups to use. It is with a huge amount of gratitude, respect, and honour we pick up the stick.

Or feather. Or shell. Choose something - something that perhaps has significance to someone already in the group, or something to do with the area in which you are meeting, or something you simply choose and then imbue with sacredness. We use a small piece of bark from the mamuku tree. It is intricately carved by nature, and it washed up in the river where we meet.

And then, as you gather, open the Circle by picking up the talking piece. Once you have said some welcomes and outlined the Rules, you can either place the piece in the middle of the group to be picked up by someone else, or pass it around the group. These two different approaches can create a different feel in the Circle.

Talking Piece

Placing the Talking Piece in the middle often means it takes several minutes before someone speaks! It can feel hard to be the first person to participate in those early gatherings (although you soon get totally comfortable with it). If your Circle is a large group, placing the talking piece in and out of the middle can make the Circle take much longer, because people need to deliberately step in to pick it up, and this movement to and from the middle can create a slightly flustered ripple in the fluidity of the Circle. However, it often leads to more reflective silence, which can be an incredibly important and beautiful thing.

Passing the talking piece around the Circle (moving either clockwise or counterclockwise) has the benefit of ensuring the momentum of the Circle continues. It can also encourage more participation from people who aren't naturally very vocal: when the piece arrives in their hands they often decide that they do want to speak after all. After someone has spoken it can be good to settle on a word to honour what the person has said, and then all say it together to acknowledge her words.

The Kiowa word "aho" is often spoken by the people sitting in circle, to honour the words just shared. "Aho" says "thank you for sharing: we have heard you."

After a lot of discussion and reflection we settled on a Māori word, as we felt it summed up more of what we wanted to get across when we breathed it out together, and we were unsure about borrowing a term from a culture with which we didn't have an association. You might like to choose your own word. "Thank You", or "We Hear You" would also work beautifully.

It is important that everyone gets to hear the Circle say "aho" (or whatever word your Circle has chosen) at the end of their sharing. The very point of the talking piece is that no one person's words are more important or resonant than another's.

Silence

Rumi says "Silence is an ocean. Speech is a river. When the ocean is searching for you, don't walk into the river. Listen to the ocean."

In the first Circle we ever held on our land we came to the fire with a reverent spirit. None of us really knew what to expect, but even as we gathered at the cars there was a sizzling sacredness sparking off our interactions with each other.

We knew we wanted to walk to the fire in silence, so we did. We knew we wanted to burn sage in silence, so we did. And then we sat down together to share and sing, but what wanted to happen was more silence!

And it was a silence that felt like an expansive, buoyant ocean. It was the opposite of awkward. It was a silence that chose us, and we knew it. It was an intentional silence. I picture that first Circle now and I see us all bobbing on the sea, all of us thinking "Yep, this sea is me right now." Except we weren't thinking anything - just being held, completely held, in a very full, very silent presence.

We spoke about it after, and tried to analyse it. Many of us are mamas, and all of us are busy folk. It struck us that we spend so much time being talked to, in conversation, and surrounded by noise. Being given the chance to sit beneath the stars, in company but completely still and quiet is probably something we all just knew we needed!

Moon Circle

I'm sure that it is that, yet it's also something more. In these long gaps, these intentional silences, we are connecting with each other and the earth, and the very moment, on a deep energy level. Soul to soul. Or something. Whatever the words are, it doesn't really matter: the whole point is that words aren't required! It is true oneness, being experienced in a group.

It's totally amazing, by the way.

So. You might have a full, wordy Circle - one that loves to sing and talk and feast. But you might have one with long silences and I say: Don't interrupt the silence. Don't short circuit it with a choked giggle or awkward shuffle. Allow yourself to be utterly sucked into it.

Remember, this ocean of silence has chosen you!

Song

Looking at the four healing salves again, I suspect that 'singing' is the hardest one to embrace. The silence, the sharing stories, and the movement seem to be somewhat free from the burden of 'expertise'. When it comes to singing we have this idea that it is something you either can do or can't do, rather than thinking of it as something that is linked to well-being!

While there is a reason some people are superstars and the rest of us can listen to their songs on repeat, raising our voices together is part of the human experience, and it doesn't NEED to sound good enough to sell on iTunes! One of my most intense collective moments - don't laugh - happened at a U2 concert in Auckland. Bono was rocking an anthem, and the whole crowd was belting it out. It wasn't pretty. It wasn't recordable. It was just a massive group of people who didn't care what they sounded like - they were just lost in the moment, off-key, quite hoarse, and yet strangely beautiful.

So many cultures have a tradition of raising their voices together in some way. My own heritage is Welsh and, wowzers, Welsh people can sing. Even when they are doing a football chant they sound like a choir. And then there are the Inuit and Icelandic singing traditions, which use guttural throat sounds other people can only dream about being able to make. I love to remember the different sounds humans can make, to challenge the pop-star singing norms that surround me. Like many societal norms, these singing norms are both pretty ethnocentric and unattainable. Let's chuck them in the bin and throw our voices together, and see what interesting sounds emerge! In the 'Activities' chapter I share a little about the Sound Circle we sometimes enjoy- if you are up for making a unique collective noise, do read that bit!

Now that we've clarified that the aim of singing in our Moon Circle is not to sound pretty, let's discuss what the point of it might be!

On a purely chemical level, singing releases endorphins - guaranteed to give us a little shot of happiness - but when you sing in a group other, mystical things happen, I'm sure of it!

There is a sacred utensil, a purerehua, used by Māori here in New Zealand, an instrument used at the start of sacred ceremonies. It's a small surfboard-shaped object on a string, and you cast it into the air and begin spinning it. It makes a rhythmic, ethereal, whirring sound. It's said that as the purerehua enters the air it carries the spirit of the player with it, and as it whirrs it sends out the dreams and desires of the player out across the Earth and into the Heavens. A Māori friend of mine, has travelled the world and found a similar tool in Aboriginal communities in Australia, and in First Nations indigenous communities. In each of the three cultures my friend has seen the instrument used as an instrument of prayer, one Aboriginal player described it as something that
"opens the doorway between heaven and earth - to slice a little opening and let some of the sacred in."

I feel like the singing part of our Circle fulfills this function for us. When we open our throats with our rough, raw, sweet, singing, we sink into this new space we have created - a space where anything can happen, where each one of us is saying yes to vulnerability, community, and healing. The sacred stuff.

Song

But what to sing?!

There might be a simple song that one of you knows from childhood, or that you've learnt recently. Do use it - how beautiful to have your own Circle song. In our Circle we tend to pull in songs from all sorts of places. We have made them up in the past if we've wanted one on a certain theme, and every now and then even Spotify throws up something that we use in Circle.

I have put together some of the songs we love and sing regularly on a Youtube playlist under my Youtube Channel Lulastic and the Hippyshake. Perhaps you could listen to some and choose one or two to bring to your Circle. Or it might be that you're more comfortable with chanting - it is useful in much the same way.

We find that there is a certain self-consciousness at the start of a song, but after singing it many times over, we fall into it more: our brains stop analysing the sound of it, and it becomes a collective, rhythmic experience that can feel tingly to sit in.

Roles and Rules

Solidarity is identifying with one another without feeling like you have to agree on every issue. It's unity, not uniformity. It's listening without rushing in to fix the problem. It's going deeper than typical ways of talking and sharing—going down to the place where souls meet and love comes, where separateness drops away and you know these women because you are these women.[10]

~

There's very few specific roles that need to be fulfilled in a Moon Circle, but the one that absolutely needs to happen is that of the hosts. The hosts will open and close the Circle, and guide the rituals and activities throughout the night. But it is the invisible stuff that goes on in-between that is the most important! The hosts are the ones who holds the space for everyone in the Circle - I'll refer to them as the 'space holder' here.

Perhaps you've been in a meeting or workshop that hasn't been held - it would have felt unsatisfactory, discordant, maybe even a bit awkward - and perhaps a little unsafe. You might have found yourself closing up rather than opening up, and chances are you will have wanted to stay quiet. A held space feels uncomfortable, but often you can't quite put your finger on why. On the other hand, a space that is held well feels like it flows - like everyone can drop into their heart zone, like silence is A Beautiful Thing.

The main thing for the hosts to do is to enter the Circle with a strong sense of intention. You might have a single word that you keep coming back to, or a phrase that you breathe in and out. The space holder holds the intention of the Circle in the forefront of her mind throughout the evening. Simply having someone whose role is guardian of the Circle is like having a rudder on the boat: they provide the safety and direction for the group to rest within. They might move the Circle on from sharing to an activity, or interject with a song suggestion or ritual if they feel it is needed. Often a space holder might not even say much at all in Circle, but occasionally they may need to help remind sitters of the importance of not giving advice.

In our Circle two of us usually hold the space, and it is usually the person who is hosting the Circle on their land or in their home. In many circles people take turns to hold the space, as it can feel quite different to sit in Circle in that role: space holders often find that they're not quite as keen to share deeply, perhaps.

It can make sense to have two hosts: one can be the person that actively moves the evening from one thing to the other; and the other can silently hold the intention - or people could partner to hold space and guide the evening together.

In the Gather the Women movement they often have a secondary space holding role: that of a bell ringer. Their job is simply to chime a small bell when it feels as though the Circle needs to be reminded to come back to sacred listening and speaking, or to mark a moment of silence when it feels necessary, or to move the Circle on to the next ritual.

Moon Circle

At the start of your Moon Circle journey it is absolutely fine to be a 'trainee' space holder! You can be really honest with your Circle about how it feels to be learning the space-holding ropes. And it might transpire eventually that some are more naturally suited to holding space than others. That is also absolutely fine.

Opening and Closing the Circle

The space-holders create a safe container for the Moon Sisters to sit within, a way for emotion and vulnerability to bubble up and provide nourishment without spilling out. The story of the Magic Porridge Pot springs to mind; we are the young girl, the old magical crone and starving villagers sitting around a cauldron of sustenance. Within the walls of the pot the porridge is pure goodness, but when it overflows it causes devastation.

A Moon Circle is a cauldron of sorts, a place for all of our fears and griefs and fantasies and dreams to be stirred up without them suffocating the other parts of our lives. One of the ways space-holders do this is by formalising the opening and closing of the Circle. It's a simple but important step. Our psyches learn to rest into everything that happens in between those opening and closing words.

We often open with a Welcome, and with the song "Home, Welcome Home" which is on my playlist mentioned in the Song chapter. And we often closed with the old sacred prayer "May the Circle be open and never broken, may the peace of the Goddess be ever in our hearts." Sometimes we sing it too. (Also on the playlist.)

I encourage you to think about how you might open and

Roles and Rules

close your circle using words, song or symbol.

Rules

Here's the thing: this isn't some patriarchal militant imperialist institution. A Moon Circle is the opposite!

There are no hierarchical rules here, merely some good principles. Here are some of the guiding principles we have in our Circle.

We borrow the first four from the Open Space community. Open Space is a tool for collective activity and organising, and is well worth looking into if you love democratic spaces.

1. Whoever come are the right people to come.
2. Whatever happens is the only thing that could have happened.
3. Whenever it starts is the right time.
4. When it's over, it's over.

These are great principles, as they allow complete trust in the Circle, who comes, and what is said. Sometimes we are all present and correct, and sometimes there are only three of us, but in every Circle we have this strong sense that it is all meant to be. We always aim to gather at 7:30pm, but sometimes we don't end up sitting until 8:30pm. Sometimes it's all over at 10pm, and other times it has been past midnight. Some friends are in a Circle that sit and feast, and sit again all night from 9pm until dawn, and the pure, perfect energy of the Circle spurs them on through school runs the following morning.

The only other principle we aim for is avoiding chatter and advice. We hold tight to it because we don't want our Circles to be like the other times we gather. We want it to be sacred: full of deep listening and deep speaking. Using the talking piece - a symbolic element we hold as we're speaking - helps us stick to this principle: to speak and listen from the heart.

This has been tricky for some people to accept: usual friendship protocol does involve a little bit of back and forth, some consoling, a similar experience, and a few wise nuggets imparted. We recently implemented a new idea, where someone can choose to invite this kind of feedback. It might be in circumstances when they have experienced something huge and want some verbal validation, or when they genuinely want to hear some guidance from the sisters they've come to hold dear. Usually this person will share last in the Circle and will, at the end of their share, ask for the kind of feedback they'd like from the group.

Unless they've asked for this feedback, we actively discourage it. If someone begins to give advice when it hasn't been asked for the Space Holder will kindly remind them that we are here to hear and hold space for our sisters, not to give them tips.

Often we don't want opinions or twenty solutions we've already considered. Sometimes all we need is to be heard, all we want is to tell our stories and share our feelings. A Moon Circle is one of the only places in our communities that we'll get to experience the sensation of being heard deeply without receiving advice. It is precious and we like to protect it.

The activities

A circle of women can provide a container for emergence in a way that a woman alone or even a one-to-one relationship cannot. Intimate relationships and even friendships can break or at least be greatly strained by life changes. But from the combined wisdom and energy of a small group of women who are committed to "hearing each other into speech," continuity and trust can develop that can be relied on over the long term. And, witnessing each person's direct knowing of her truth, we can be empowered to live our own.[11]

~

Some groups might keep a fairly simple Circle - an opening ritual, followed by a sharing circle. We like to do all that AND a couple of other activities! Some of these we love so much we do them each time, and others we have done once and they've been magical. And of course there are many other activities we haven't done, but will be open towards. Keep your eyes and ears open for connecting activities that strike you as being something you'd like to experience, and then bring them into the Circle to see if people would like to try them with you.

Choosing an object

Sometimes we pass around a basket of shells, or items from nature, or beads. We ask people to thoughtfully choose one.

Moon Circle

Once the basket has gone around the Circle people are invited to share why they think that particular object spoke to them. It becomes a leaping off point for something that might have been buried deep within our minds. Sometimes we begin with one thing - "The pink in the shell reminded me of the shell I used to collect from the beach with my Nana" - and end up somewhere quite important - "sometimes I wish I could be that little girl, unburdened, whizzing in and out of the tide looking for sparkly things."

Hand massage

At one beautiful Circle last winter a member brought some hand cream she had made. We paired up and passed the cream around, and gave each other hand massages. None of us were expert as massage therapists, but we just gently rubbed the cream into each other's hands. We were mostly silent, and it felt luxurious to show kindness to each other through touch.

With no planning - simply rolling with the theme - we began sharing stories about our hands. We shared the unexpected things our hands had done, and the hopes we held for our hands - what we dream our hands might one day do.

The gaze

One of the first 'bold' activities we attempted involved pairing up and sitting opposite each other, and staring for two minutes into each other's eyes. One person sat out, in order to keep track of time, and, when the two minutes were up, we swapped pairs, so eventually everyone had stared into each other's eyes. It felt good to have one person sitting out, almost as if they were holding the space for us - it gave a sense of safety in what was quite a vulnerable exercise. There were a few giggles the first time we did this activity, but they were quickly absorbed into the power of the moment. It brought up of different things for different people - from the practical *"I realised how little I really make eye contact with people"* to the revealing *"I felt a sense of shame, being stared at so intensely"* to the celestial *"I felt a soul to soul connection."* . Each revelation gave much pause for thought and a chance to delve deeper into consciousness.

We also found ourselves able to share pictures that sprang into our minds as we stared - these were sometimes received hungrily by the recipient, as though the visions had really struck a chord.

Touch

Recently I sat in circle with a woman called Jaguar Star of the Women's School. It was a different experience for me as all the women were strangers, but it was absolutely beautiful and I felt like I was gifted with quite a few insights to treasure.

At the start of the circle we paired up and began the activity I've called "The Gaze" above. Then she asked us, if we felt comfortable, to begin showing physical affection to the other woman. She asked us to gently stoked the other person's hands, and she guided us through it with her words: through your touch, let her know she is welcome here, stroke her arms with kindness, that she might feel she is valued and loved. My partner and I had tears rolling down our faces as we stroked each other's hands, arms and shoulders.

It was an incredibly moving experience, and it made me realise how much I had missed female affection! When I was a child and a teenager my friends and I were always touching each other - hugging or draping ourselves over each other. We even fell asleep cuddling. Since being an adult almost all affection has been either as a lover or a mother. I was also struck by how much the world would have us believe women are not for each other, that we don't care for each other. Caring for each other with our kind touch was a potent panacea.

I came away understanding a small need within myself, and also wanting to give energy to this idea that women have each other's backs.

Embodied listening

Every now and then we enter a really deep collective experience, where we quieten our hearts and speak out loud what we experience within our bodies. Each time we have done this we have moved quickly into a zone that feels far bigger than ourselves, it has felt as though we've found helpful pictures together - symbols and stories that seem to have been a gift to us.

So it might begin: "I feel a heaviness in my legs." And someone else might immediately say "There is tension in my shoulders." And another: "I am sinking into the ground." "I feel light, as if I am floating." "I feel strong, as though we have climbed a mountain." "I feel my heart thumping, I feel excited."

It's almost impossible to describe what it is like, as each time has been quite different. Sometimes it is like we are all feeling the same thing, and other times it feels as though we are experiencing opposite responses. Suze, the friend who has brought this activity to our Circle has facilitated this experience many times before, and assures us that this is normal! Every now and then she reminds us to come back to how it feels bodily, to just speak out loud the sensations in our body.

Suze describes this activity as tapping into the river of womanhood: an energetic movement of our histories, experience, and wisdom that is always there, just below the surface. It has certainly felt like that at times, as though we are listening in to something wise beyond our Circle. You can find out more about Embodied Wholeness from Suze's site SusanDurcan.com[12]

Heart to heart listening

We have also taking The Gaze activity a little deeper by pairing up and deep listening to each other. Sometimes this might involve eye contact, but it's often nice to just hold hands and close eyes. We sit for a couple of minutes, trying to connect on a heart to heart level, to try and hear some words or get a picture for something that person might need.

It's been incredibly powerful! There have been images and words that have been spot on. But we have all found the exercise to be an incredibly bold act of trusting oneself. We all come away feeling much more able to trust ourselves, and to speak out loud what our heart might be telling us.

Sound Circle

Sometimes we have a sense that we want to do something a bit more... unusual. When this is the case we often do a Sound Circle. It's when you begin making sounds together: any sound, whatever comes out, it will all do just perfectly! There is a healing tradition of toning - this is when you all chime in with a long, single note, keeping it going, and sometimes harmonising with it. It's a really beautiful form of Circling together. Our Sound Circles are different though: they cover a range of notes and use the voice box in any way that suits the women taking part. Sometimes we make wonderful harmonised sounds together, bouncing off each other and getting louder and quieter in an amazing show of musical accomplishment, despite only one or two of us being very musically accomplished! It's not the aim though. There is no aim to sound nice. The aim is for every woman to feel free to use her voice in any way she wants to - to represent her feelings in her sounding.

It's actually incredibly liberating and vulnerable, and leaves me feeling brave enough to roar out the truth I have - even if it's ugly to people!

It's also one of those activities where afterwards, when I'm lying in bed, I might wonder if the neighbours heard us.

Honouring Circle

Did you ever do that thing in high school where you put a piece of paper on your back, and then all your classmates go around writing the things they like about each other on the piece of paper? An honouring circle is like that! But without the paper, and one by one! People can simply say "I've been having such a rough time lately, I would love to sit in the middle tonight", or you might all take it in turns one evening to sit in the middle.

It's a chance to peacefully sit together and say out loud the things you love and value about the person in the middle. It runs deeper than words, too. The act of sitting at the centre of a powerful group of women who love you can be incredibly transformative.

Crowning

On the Circle we held at Beltane, the festival of fertility that happens in the spring, we brought out a beautiful bushy fern and flower crown. At certain points throughout the evening the crown was passed from one woman to another, as a way of honouring something she'd shared about. One woman received the crown after describing a new phase of creativity she was entering. Another woman received it as she shared the anticipation she felt about a new project she was launching. We blessed them with a prayer of fruitfulness, and I found it filled my heart to see my sisters looking so much like some Harvest Goddess of Abundance. (I made that Goddess up...)

Honouring Life's Transitions

One of the really wonderful things that a moon circle provides is a community of women at different stages of their life. We can begin to reclaim those stages, to provide rituals for those transitioning from one stage to another. I was recently in a Circle with an older woman, an elder of our community, who felt unable to move into her 'cronehood' (a respectful term of honour for those wiser, powerful years as a woman). A friend led a beautiful ritual one candlelit night in the forest, where our older friend was called into her cronehood. It involved her sharing her thoughts on her life, and revisiting the parts of her last stage that were joyful or hard. She shared how she was feeling about the new stage she was entering. She then physically stood and walked to a new part of the circle, where those representing cronehood were standing. We were then all able to greet her in her new role and share some tea together. It was powerful for her, and the next day she felt like a new woman! She even looked like a new woman - fresh and bold, and standing tall. She had been stuck, unable to move forward, and this small ceremony made her feel welcome in the new phase of her life.

While there are plenty of rituals out there (a quick Google will give you some ideas), I believe these transitions are best marked with authentic, heartfelt rituals created by communities of women themselves. For example: if some, or one, of you want to honour menopause, or want to retroactively honour a previous transition (such as menarche - your first bleed), you could sit down together and talk about how a ritual might look for you. It might involve you honouring the phase you were in before, either with words or symbolically. And it will involve you moving into your new phase, either physically or symbolically. It might involve objects or songs that represent the different phases. It might take ten minutes or involve an hour-long ceremony.

Other friends had sat in a circle together for a long time before they noticed an ache around the fact that their own first bleed went by without any sort of ritual or honouring. So they decided to create a ceremony that honoured their first bleed, even though many of them were mothers by then and their first bleed was decades ago. The ritual they created involved them wearing items of clothing that represented the pre-menarche them, and then walking along a pathway and greeting a mentor (of their choosing) who welcomed them into womanhood.

I love this idea of creating new ways to honour life's transitions. It's common to borrow from other cultures and do a fairly poor job of it! Instead, why not bring our own imagination and creativity together to mark the things we want to commemorate?

Fire

We dare not talk of the darkness
for fear it will infect us.
We dare not talk of the fire,
for fear it will destroy us.
And so we live in the half-light,
Like our mothers before us.

Come to the fire,
Feel it warm your skin.
Come to the fire,
Feel it burn in your belly,
Shine out through your eyes.
Come dance in the fire,
Let it fuel your prayers.[13]

~

We love having our Moon Circles around the fire. I'll
not lie - every time I make a fire, building it in my own special
way (a way that I know Boy Scouts would sniff at), I feel like a
bit of a rock star: cavewoman edition. There's something
powerful about raising fire from a couple of toilet rolls and some
twigs. (And one of those lighters with the loooong pointy snout.)

We often meet at the cars and walk across the meadow to
the fire, the beacon of warmth drawing us in.

The fire allows us to make a room out of any place. Our
Circles move around our farm each month, from the river to the

forest, or to another person's garden, but always there tends to be the fire around which we sit. We burn things in it that we want to get rid of. We light candles from it when we are marking something important.*

The fire keeps us warm on those cold winter nights when our stories are shared on the white mist of our breath, and there are nights that are punctuated with long silences as the flames seem to mesmerise us, as they stir up memories and feelings that don't have to be spoken out loud.

The fire is our hearth as we plant ourselves amongst nature, and I don't think it's a coincidence that, parallel to my awakening to my sisters through Moon Circles, there's been an awakening to the earth. One night we stumbled deep into the forest, where we'd set up a little space with blankets, cushions, flowers, and candles. Throughout our Circle there were strange creakings and scratchings, and the odd squeal coming from the edges. All around us we heard the weird scrape of the native weta: a huge, gnarly looking bug that is so dense that when it climbs trees it sounds like a groaning of sorts, and we all shuffled in a little closer. The forest was alive and we were alive in it - just a few extras amongst the community of nature. As the night darkened, the trees around us began to glow, as if we were looking straight on at the Milky Way, but even brighter. Actually, it was more as though someone had snuck in and decorated the whole place in tiny fairy lights. But they were glow worms, spinning away as they do every night, usually out of sight. We were reverent, in awe that these tiny creature could create a space so spectacular, and that we could share it with them.

In her book *If Women Rose Rooted* Sharon Blackie wrote:

Fire

"We spend our lives searching for meaning in ourselves, engaged in deep conversations with our 'inner child', meditating on a mat indoors, trained to be ever-mindful of what's going on inside us –our breath and our thoughts and emotions –when so much of the meaning we need is beneath our feet, in the plants and animals around us, in the air we breathe. We swaddle ourselves so tightly in the centrality of our own self-referential humanness that we forget that we are creatures of the Earth, and need also to connect with the land. We need to get out of the confines of our own heads. We need –we badly need –grounding; we need to find our anchor in place, wherever it is that we live. Once we find that anchor, so many of our problems fade away. And once we find that anchor, so often we uncover the nature of our true work, the nature of the gift we can offer up to the world."[14]

Gathering in the outdoors is one way we can embed ourselves in nature. It's a potent activity: gathering with our sisters in the wild. It's knowing ourselves anew, and understanding that we belong here, in this community of women, in this community of all living things.

Even more than simply this visceral experience of connecting with our primitive side and grounding ourselves in the earth around us, there's a symbolic element to gathering around a fire. In her book *Burning Woman* Lucy H. Pearce explores the way women carry the fear of being burned, a cultural baggage of having been thrown in the fire, at time literally, throughout history. We allow this fear to keep us small - to choose safety over rejection or pain.

Moon Circles are a place for laying down these historical burdens and picking up courage. They are the place where

Moon Circle

women sit, each with the Olympic torch of her dreams in her hands, the flame being passed from baton to baton, until all of our hopes are ignited. We are invited to raise our fiery torches, to dance in the inferno, and to burn brightly and audaciously.

~

But I don't have a meadow where I can light a fire, c'mon!
There might be a small meadow of sorts available to you though. Perhaps you could Circle together on a public heath or in a reserve, this might seem outrageous but sometimes the most public of places can be the most private; there can be a shroud of anonymity in shared public places. I wouldn't suggest you light a fire, but rather create an altar in the centre with candles, beautiful found objects from nature, photos of your heroes, flowers, or piles of gold coins. (I jest.) Or perhaps there is another place you could consider. Don't discount a fire just because you are in a built-up area: we visited friends recently in the very urban town of Luton, who had a tiny backyard and the perfect concrete square for a brazier.

To be clear, a Moon Circle doesn't hinge on being outdoors around a fire, it has just been an unexpected great joy to us. You might decide not to even meet outside! On very rainy evenings we have had wonderful Moon Circle indoors. We have lit candles and created an altar, and nurtured a sense of sacred space by washing our hands before we enter. If you choose to do this, perhaps you might go on a journey with the earth in other ways - doing specific activities outdoors, going on an occasional night walk, taking an overnight camping trip together. This is your Circle and you are going to journey into wildness your own magical way.

Blood

Her blood is the flood of life
    Redthread woven
    From victim to hero
    From minstrel to rockstar
    From doctor to gardener.
    Healing puddle
    Vat of wine
    Holy, fertile,
    Leaking.

    God caused my womb to roar so!
    To rock this boat with my blood flow!
    To disappear into my own silent glow

    for three sacred days.

    I fill my cup
    And carry it, like a treasure,
    To the ground.
    I pour it out
    That it might bloom
    Red rose sewn
    From earth to womb
    Womb to earth
    Sewn.

    ~

I was 33 years old before I began recording my moon cycle. I didn't come to it from even a vague sense of what was going on. I started with an almost total dearth of knowledge. I was 14 when I first went on the pill, and stayed on it for five years, took a small break, long enough to feel like I was doing the hard yards with painful, angry bleeds, then went on the mini pill for a further three years. I would munch my pills everyday, gleefully skipping bleeds, sticking my finger up at those old rages that used to blaze each month, and not associating my general malaise or low libido with the pill.

Then we decided to get pregnant. I was in my mid-twenties, and I discovered a thing called ovulation. I remember calling a friend and being like "Do you know you can actually only get pregnant for a few days a month?!" I'm embarrassed now by how much of a revelation it was. It didn't really help with getting pregnant though: it was either my Polycystic Ovaries Syndrome or the years on the pill that stretched out our 'trying-to-conceive' phase to a tearful, shame-filled three years.

So, pregnant, then breastfeeding, then pregnant and breastfeeding again, and I was 32 before I had another cycle. This time I was more into my body: curious about it, especially about the mysterious and ridiculously awesome parts of it. I began applying the same understanding to menstruation as I had to other parts of my body. This understanding was that the body is, by and large, quite good at doing what it does. If it does something, it is probably for a reason, and I should find out what the reason is! This logic had ended up making me a bit of a poster girl for the shampoo-free movement: I'd set out to discover why our bodies produce so much sebum, and why we get locked into shampooing every day. And I'd learnt that our hair can thrive without shampoo if we are willing to work with our body's natural processes.

Blood

I began to wonder about periods, about hormones, about my moods and body aches. My periods had come back with a vengeance, and they propelled me into the herbalist for a tincture to soften the blows of PMS, and into the library to read everything I could about women and bleeding!

Eventually this brought me to the work of The Red School in the UK, and in particular their recent book *Wild Power*.

Wild Power is an invitation to every woman to look anew at menstruation: to record their cycle; to observe their feelings; and to begin to work with the menstruation seasons. Reading *Wild Power* was like the culmination of this last year's menstruation journey, and now that I can embrace each element of my cycle. I find myself looking forward to the parts that used to be hard, because I know that when impatience and intolerance gurgles in my belly, my mind is at its most lucid, and my soul is getting ready to enter this state of weird, visionary power.

I explain all this because it adds to the texture of our Moon Circle. It partly explains why it is a Moon Circle and not just a gathering of friends at the pub or in a lounge. The moon plays a role, and our menstruation plays a role. There is a shared understanding that when we meet together on a New Moon we are reclaiming something: a connection between these two cycles, and a long lost knowledge that has been erased from history.

Sometimes we begin our Circle by sharing where we are in our menstruation cycle as a way of honouring it. Sometimes we plot ourselves around the circle accordingly. I recently read of a women's circle where participants bought some of the blood they'd saved from menstruation, and used it for rituals.

Moon Circle

Moon Circles are the ideal place for women to begin to gather knowledge of their bodies, to share this wisdom with each other, and to honour the different stages of a woman's menstrual life. They are the place we can help women transition through menopause, where we can celebrate young women's first bleeds, and where we can retrospectively honour our own first bleed.

These days I use a menstrual cup, and I love how it connects me to my bleed in such a visceral way. I collect my blood in a teapot: a very specific teapot that I keep in the bathroom. It's vintage, with gold stripes and colourful juggling clowns. So if you ever come over for a cuppa when I'm old and have lost my marbles and I begin pouring tea with the gold striped, colourful clown teapot feel free to say "Excuse me, Lucy, I believe that for many years you used this as a vestibule for your menses, shall we use a different pot today, friend?"

Once I've collected it in a teapot and mixed it with water, I pour it on my flowers. And as I do, I always find myself thinking of my Moon Circle sisters, and the wider tide of womanhood, and all the ways in which I grow out of the earth.

It's for you and your Circle to decide how explicitly you want to bring your menstrual cycles in, but whatever you decide, I encourage you to find this body wisdom available to us those of us with menstrual cycles. Not all women have them, some are passed that phase and some women will never bleed, so there is also some sensitivity required here.

Moon

Everyone is a moon, and has a dark side which he never shows to anybody.[15]

~

What's the moon got to do with it, got to do with it, got to do with it?

(Prizes to whoever guessed I was singing that in my best Tina Turner voice!)

One of the unexpected bonuses of a Moon Circle has been getting the rhythm of the moon into my life. In the past I've barely even noticed whether the moon is waxing or waning: these days I have just as much awareness of the moon stages as I do the numbers on the calendar.

Ancient wisdom suggests that women traditionally bleed in a new moon phase, and ovulate in a full moon phase. Charles Darwin thought so too, and there've been a few studies to suggest this might be the case. There's also been research to show there isn't a correlation, and Circles that I've sat in have tended to show little correlation between the moon stages and the menstrual cycle of the women present.

Once I began tracking my menstrual cycles I found that when the moon disappears and then comes as a sliver I know I'm about to bleed hard, or enter a state where I am getting great insight from daydreams. This sense of living under the moonbeams is a cool glass of water to me: I never really knew I needed it until I realise how refreshed I am through it. I wonder if it differs from person to person, perhaps even according to the stage of life they are in, or the place they live, or perhaps there has been a Great Unsyncing between our wombs and the moon as we've into a stage of civilisation that removes us from the wild places and lunar beams.

However, while we might not know objectively whether the moon directly guides menstruation, we can understand that there is a magical relationship between the moon and our menstruations, as evidenced in the four phases of both.

The moon has a phase of waning (getting darker), and then being dark, and then waxing (getting lighter), and then being bright. A woman's menstrual cycle mirrors this waxing and waning. In the lead up to bleeding we often feel energetically lower, quieter, and reflective, and then we have quite a strong dark phase as we bleed. Once we have bled we grow increasingly open, brighter, more sociable, and more energetic, until we ovulate when we are at our most dynamic and full. We then begin the cycle again.

In some women the lunar cycles and menstrual cycles are in sync, making them quite intense. For other women there might be a little overlap, and others might find that their moods are affected more strongly by the lunar rhythms than by their menstrual cycle.

We tend to have our Circle on the Tuesday closest to the New Moon each month. It seems harder to psych ourselves up - we often text back and forth, do we feel like it? Can we be bothered? But then once we are there we are always SO glad to

Moon

be there. We find it easy to drop into this deep, reflective zone, as if the dark of the moon has invited us into our shadow selves. Although we are friends now, it is easy to resist the jokes and giggles: we are only ever a ritual away from revealing our most vulnerable sides to each other.

We can be so afraid of this dark side: so unwilling to reveal our betrayals, our anger, our depression, and our meanness. When we only show our bright moon face to our community we perpetuate this crippling idea that everyone is awesome, doing great, happy, and fulfilled... apart from me. When we are able to share the cross days and the disappointments we give room for belonging to blossom, because we are unveiling the truth.

Everyone is awesome. And every one sucks. Everyone has legendary days, and everyone has days when they regret getting out of bed. But, despite all this, there is a place for us. We are loved. We belong.

Recently we had our Circle on a Full Moon, and even as we were sitting in circle at 11pm it felt as bright as the day. It was wonderful to be out on such a lit-up night - a great pleasure. Somehow we ended up on our backs, watching the moon cast colourful moonbows across the fairytale clouds. We shared from our hearts that night, but there was also much distraction and laughter - it wasn't as easy to keep the songs going until they became transcendental: we were almost too buoyant to become deeply grounded in sacredness. It made us decide to have joyful seasonal celebrations on a Full Moon, but keep our deep sharing circles on a New Moon.

Practicalities

Body, earth
Blood, dirt
Holy, complete
Formed, whole
I am woman
I give birth to land
To oceans and mountains
Forest and vale
See me in the hills
Wise eyes in the rock
Watching you
Shape piles of shit
Into myth
(Were I to crumble
You would be dust.)

~

    This might seem like a bit of a mundane chapter, but I really do want to provide you with a useful resource, so you can start your own Moon Circle. I hope you've also found a lot of practical bits of information embedded in the other chapters, but here's some extra tidbits that might be helpful.

Finding the best night of the week
    Once you have a small bunch of interested women an online meeting scheduler can help you figure out which night of the week is going to work best. I like a tool called Doodle Poll, which you can find via Google.

Practicalities

Reminder emails

At the start of each year I check the calendar and figure out which Tuesday night is closest to the New Moon. I then email the list of dates to everybody, so they can pencil them in. Another woman from the Circle sends a reminder email a few days before the scheduled date, to make sure we all remember. I like that we share this responsibility, as I'm rubbish at that sort of upkeep!

Food

Lots of circles either start or end with a meal. Ideally this is easy 'pot luck' style food: everyone brings a dish to share (one that doesn't need heating), and everyone helps to clear up.

What to have
Candles
Talking Piece
Flowers/ object for an altar or centrepiece
Cushions or seating of some kind
Tissues, just in case
Herbs or oils for burning
A book of meditations or poetry (this can often be useful to draw on)
A drum or two can help add to the singing

What people should bring
We meet outside around a fire, so people usually bring blankets, warm clothes, and wood to contribute. Otherwise, people can just bring themselves.

A Moon Circle Agenda
I thought it would be helpful to provide you with an overview of how our Moon Circles unfold. It's slightly tricky as

Moon Circle

every Circle is quite different and we also allow for it to evolve organically on the night, with lots of room to respond if something heavy comes up for someone, or we are all feeling the need for something that wasn't planned or hasn't been done before.

Of course, there are hundreds if not thousands of Circles all over the world, and this is just ours, our little fly-by-the-sacred-seat-of-our-intuitive-pants Circle. Every Circle is different and will reflect the needs of the group. We have found a deep appreciation for sitting meditatively in silence, so we do that quite a lot - but this might not resonate with your Circle.

7:30pm − 8:00pm: Gather at the cars and silent walk to the fire; smoke cleanse as our first ritual.

8:00pm - 8:30pm: Open with singing for five − ten minutes, sitting in silence; someone might lead a meditation or some yoga stretches.

8:30pm- 10:00 pm: A sharing circle - people speak and listen from the heart as we pass the stick around.

10:00pm - 10:30 pm: Deep listening; embodied womanhood activity; or sound circle activity.

10:30pm- 10:45 pm: Close with a song, or another mindful closing ritual.

Conclusion

My Moon Sister sat across from me, her face reflecting the glow of the fire. Perched on her head was an abundant crown made of ferns. It was giant sized - not an Instagram-worthy floral crown, but a verging on the ridiculous, a larger than life blaze of greenery. She'd just told us some heavy life news: news laced with the hope of a new creative stage, with the stirrings of wild adventure beckoning. We all felt we wanted to honour her, to heap blessings of courage and grace over her, so we placed the crown on her head - a small offering, but symbolic. We marked this transition with her, and prayed that it would be as fertile as the new sprigs of life curling out from the ferns on her head.

My friend wore the crown and said she'd never known she could be in a community of women like this. She'd been hurt when she was younger, and always believed that women didn't relate in supportive, encouraging ways. We began to speak out loud the myths people had tried to make us believe - that women were catty, bitchy, competitive. That there was only space for *some* women, not *all* women. That we didn't really belong. That we deserved less. That we should be quiet, respectable. Be good mothers, or, at least, nurturing. That there is no such thing, really, as *sisterhood.*

We sat for a while, still stinging from the wounds we'd lived with when we thought these myths were true. The fire flickered: someone dropped another log onto it. I felt angry that I'd lived under these myths for so long - I felt a grief for those wasted years when I thought my meaning came from men, being seen by the Male Gaze, only worshipping the Father and the Son and the (somehow male) Holy Ghost.

Moon Circle

We then spoke out loud the truth we'd come to know through our Moon Circle. Truth that our daughters know, but that is lost as they get older: that girl tribes give us life. That there is space in the world for every woman's hopes to be realised. That women are *for* each other. That we are amazing at supporting each other's dreams. That we all belong. That we can be quiet and nurturing, but we can be loud and messy and ambitious too. That we are a sisterhood.

Our Moon Circles has given us the opportunity to be in a girl tribe again. It's given us the safe place we need to get to know ourselves anew, to learn to trust our instincts and our voices again. To bravely step out of our comfort zones, to try new things, to relate in different ways, to relate in deep, deep ways. Through our Moon Circle we have come to revere ourselves, the earth, and each other. We've been freed up to step into our power. We've come to understand that we belong here.

To respect and revere ourselves, and so to bring about a world in which women are respected and revered, recognised once again as holding the life-giving power of the Earth itself. We can reclaim that image in each of us: the creative, ecstatic, powerful feminine that each of us embodies in our own unique way. Lacking it, it is no wonder that we are grieving, alienated, imbalanced – that we cannot find a way to belong to a world which denies us permission to be what we are, and which teaches us to cover up not just our bodies but our feelings, our dreams, our intuition. There comes a point in each of our lives when we face a choice. Will we stay as we are, embracing the pale shadow of womanhood permitted us by the patriarchy? Or will we sink deep into the heart of the bog, and find out what it is to reclaim our creative power as women?[16]

Conclusion

After my neighbour and I have seen everyone to their cars and walked back to the rickety bridge where we take the paths to our separate homes, we stand for a while, still feeling the glow from the evening. We do this most Circles, just gathering ourselves in the pitch blackness of a New Moon night before going to bed. Far too frequently to be believable, we see shooting stars in those minutes, blasting across the dark canvas of the night sky. I feel those stars as all the women of the past: all the forgotten women whose names we've spoken in our matriarchal lineage; all their dreams and accomplishments, adventures and feats that go unmentioned in the history books; all the women made small and timid by the patriarchy; all the daughters forced to lose touch with their wildness; all the mothers who choked their intuition; all those who cut their ties to the sisterhood of women. I see them in those stars as they strike paths across the sky and I feel them like a knowing wink and I hear them as a cheering crowd; we've finally found the thing we were meant to have all along, the Circle of sisters all women should belong to.

The next time you are out late on a New Moon, if you peer at the milky way and squint a little, you'll see an invitation written in the stars. It's an invite to wildness and belonging, an epistle to your heart, signed by the cosmos.

Acknowledgements

So many thanks to the circle of women that have held me over the last year and a half; Rebekah, Trish, Suze, Charade, Rae, Nina, and Rachel. They are inspiring lovers, mothers, and makers and they are my Moon Sisters.

And to my daughters Ramona and Juno, who are so audaciously at home in themselves. They strip naked to dance in the rain, roar in inappropriate places, and colour in their veins with felt tips if they feel like it. I hope I can be like you two one day.

Big thanks to my online community of writers, who are brilliant and amazing, and especially to Jacquelyn Collins, who gave her time to editing and proofing *Moon Circle*.

So many thanks to my Patreons, who made this book happen! Sono, Esther, Lisa, Lucy, Jo, Mishelle, Lauren Joanne, Betsy, Arathi, Cynthia, Laurie, Melanie, Adam, Rachel, Kumari, Amz, Franziska, Sarah, Lianne, Hope, Bobbie, Claire, Rachel, Liz, Tessa, Jenny, Danielle, Zoe, Angela, Monica, Morgan, AmberLouise, Sarah, Lisa, Cate, Haley, Rebecca, Rebecca, Eleanor, Justine, Hayley, Leanne, Stacey, Deborah, Jo, Beth, Alison, Carolyn, Santam, Rachel, Jenny, Ruth, Sophie, Anna, Melissa, Kellie, Kathryn, Jo, Hannah, Charis, Xanthe, Meriel, Katrina, Laura, Elizabeth, Amy, Jinti, Lisa, Andrea, AManda, Laura, Viv, Bryony, Janine, Sarah, Gemma, Sara, Rebecca, Melanie, Sharma, Sendy, Gary, Exploring, Celeste, Caitrin, Montse, Anna, Kesha, Ratna, Nicola, Eloise, Becky, Anneliese, Dani, Nicole, Loona, Amber, Sian, Demmaree, Lucy, Sarah,

Acknowledgements

Raelene, Kay, Waiting, Natalie, Melanie, Penny, Becky, Eva, Danielle, Allan, Melanie, Jenna, Rachel Louise, Victoria- you guys blow me away with your support and I am deeply grateful for you.

Endnotes

[1] http://www.jeanshinodabolen.com/

[2] . http://www.womboflight.com/why-its-crucial-for-women-to-heal-the-mother-wound/

[3] . http://www.mum.org/MenstHut.htm

[4] . Monk Kidd, S. (1996) Dance of the Dissident Daughter, New York: Harper Collins

[5] . Jacobs, A.J., (2007) A year of living biblically, New York: Simon and Schuster

[6] . Gilbert, E. (2006) Eat, Pray, Love Bloomsbury: London

[7] . https://inaliminalspace.org/about-us/what-is-a-liminal-space/

[8] . Arrien, A., (!993) The Four Fold Way, Harpercollins, New York

[9] . Baldwin, C., (2005) Storycatcher: making sense of our lives through the power and practice of story, New World Library, Novato

[10] Monk Kidd, S. (1996) Dance of the Dissident Daughter, New York: Harper Collins

[11] Anderson, S.R. and Hopkins, P. (2010) The Feminine Face of God; Bantam Press

[12] . http://www.susandurcan.com/

[13] . Pearce, L.H., (2016) Burning Woman, Womancraft Publishing

[14] . Blackie, S. (2016) if women rose rooted, September Publishing

[15] Mark Twain

[16] . Blackie, S. (2016) if women rose rooted, September

Endnotes

Publishing

Made in the USA
Middletown, DE
04 June 2024

55258073R00047